W.B. YEATS
Poet and Patriot

Written by Tina Callaghan
Illustrated by Derry Dillon

POOLBEG

Published 2018
Poolbeg Press Ltd

123 Grange Hill, Baldoyle
Dublin 13, Ireland

Text © Poolbeg Press Ltd 2018

ISBN 978 1 78199 788 8

Cover design and illustrations by Derry Dillon
Printed by KC Print, Killarney

William Butler Yeats, known to his family as Willie, was born on the 13th of June 1865 in Sandymount, Dublin. He lived to 1939, the very brink of World War II, having witnessed all the political and cultural upheaval of Ireland's struggle for independence. He has been called the 'spearhead' of the Irish Literary Revival. He served two terms as a Senator in the new Irish government after the establishment of the Irish Free State.

In 1923, he was the first Irishman to be awarded the Nobel Prize in Literature.

Today, his poetry is taught in schools and universities worldwide and is an integral part of Irish culture and the Irish literary tradition. William Butler Yeats is a poet of truly international acclaim.

Sligo Roots

William's father, John Butler Yeats, came from County Down and was a graduate of Trinity College Dublin. His mother, Susan Mary Pollexfen, was the daughter of a well-to-do merchant and seafaring family in Sligo on the west coast of Ireland.

The Pollexfens were a well-off Protestant family, who nevertheless were ranked below the 'Big House' Anglo Irish families such as the Gore-Booths of Lissadell. The Anglo-Irish were the Irish upper class. Protestant and educated, they were the descendants of English settlers, and had controlled the political, social and cultural life of Ireland

for centuries. William was proud of his own Protestant heritage and the role Protestants had played in culture and politics in Ireland, yet he admitted: "We were merchant people of the town. No matter how rich we became ... we could never be 'county', nor indeed did we have any desire to be so.'

In later years John Butler Yeats said that he had never really loved his wife Susan, that their marriage was 'just destiny'. In marrying her he had given 'a tongue to the sea-cliffs', he said, apparently referring to Susan's love of Sligo, its folklore and landscape, and its influence on his eloquent son William.

Susan's family thought that she was marrying a solicitor, but John was more attracted to the world of art. Two years after William's birth he abandoned his career as a solicitor and took up painting, entering the Heatherley School of Fine Art in London, taking his family there with him. He eventually became a well-known portrait artist, painting many of the prominent members of Irish political and literary life, but he was not good with money and the family always struggled.

The Yeats household was a creative one, with William's father, brother and two sisters all artists of one kind or another. Jack Butler Yeats was six years younger than his poet brother and is among Ireland's most famous artists. He loved to paint the West of Ireland and among his favourite subjects were horses and the sea. Their two sisters, Susan and Elizabeth (known as Lily and Lolly), were talented printmakers.

After William was born, the family moved to the Pollexfen home at Merville, Sligo, to stay with Susan's family. Though the family moved to London when William was two, the children spent their holidays in Sligo every summer. And so, as Yeats grew up, he had Sligo's rugged landscape, folklore and history to influence him. It always, for him, was the 'country of the heart', as expressed in his much-loved poem 'The Lake Isle of Innisfree':

I will arise and go now, for always night and day
I hear lake water lapping with low sounds by the shore;
While I stand on the roadway, or on the pavements grey,
I hear it in the deep heart's core.

City Life

When William was 7 years old, Susan and the children moved back to Sligo, where they spent two years from 1872 to 1874. After this they returned to London to John who had finished his artistic training. Susan was miserable in London – she hated city life and desperately missed Sligo.

At first, the children were educated at home, learning from their mother's storytelling and her love of folklore. Their father taught them some geography, chemistry and history. In 1877, at the age of 12, William went to the Godolphin School in London, where he spent four years, without standing out in any way.

In late 1881, for financial reasons, the family moved back to Dublin, where 16-year-old William enrolled in Erasmus Smith High School. He spent a lot of time in his father's art studio and met many of his artist and writer friends. William started to write poetry during this time.

Poetry and Magic

In 1884 William began to attend the Metropolitan School of Art and his first poems were published by the Dublin University Review in 1885 when he was 20.

From his early years, largely because of his mother's influence, William had been interested in folktales and the occult. During his time at the School of Art, his friendship with George Russell, who wrote poetry under the pseudonym AE, led him to pursue his interest in Irish mythology, the occult and mysticism.

William left college in 1886, and the following year the Yeats family moved back to London where he met many great writers and society figures. Among them was the Russian occultist Madame Blavatsky who had just set up the Theosophist Society which explored mysticism and the supernatural. William joined the society and experimented with the practice of magic.

In 1889, he published his first major book of poetry, *The Wanderings of Oisin and Other Poems* and was immediately recognised as a significant poet. The title poem is an epic where the mythical Irish hero Oisín tells the story of his former life in the Isles of Faerie. However, it is the lyrical poems in the collection that have stood the test of time and become classic Yeats. Perhaps typical is the haunting 'The Stolen Child'. Informed by folklore, dreamlike and romantic, Yeats' poem also has roots in the real world in his vivid and precise nature imagery.

Where dips the rocky highland
Of Sleuth Wood in the lake,
There lies a leafy island
Where flapping herons wake
The drowsy water rats;
There we've hid our faery vats,
Full of berry
And of reddest stolen cherries.
Come away, O human child!
To the waters and the wild
With a faery, hand in hand.
For the world's more full of weeping
than you can understand.

Meeting his Muse

The year 1889 was also the year that William, aged 24, met the person who was to be his greatest muse, both for his poetry and his dramatic works. He met the beautiful, enigmatic Maud Gonne.

Six-foot-tall, English-born Maud was 22 years old. After her mother died when she was only 5 years old, Maud was sent to France to be educated. Then in 1882 her father, an army officer, had been posted to Dublin and she had accompanied him. The Gonne family had roots in both Scotland and Ireland, and Maud seized on the Irish part of her identity and quickly became a passionate Irish nationalist. She actively agitated for Home Rule for Ireland and feminist causes and was outspoken and independent.

To Yeats, the dreamer and mystic, she was the living embodiment of everything he had ever wanted. After they met in London and spent a few days in each other's company, he fell madly in love with her, although she did not share his feelings. She was having a relationship with a French journalist and right-wing politician named Lucien Millevoye with whom she eventually had two children. Georges was born in 1890 and died the following year, a tragedy Maud never really recovered from, and Iseult was born in 1894. Maud and Yeats were destined to be linked for a long time. Her spirit, beauty and his passion for her were the subject of many of his poems and plays.

The Golden Dawn

In 1890, aged 25, Yeats joined the Hermetic Order of the Golden Dawn. In the same year he was asked to leave the Theosophist Society because of his experiments in practical magic, which didn't suit the society's philosophy.

Yeats was not alone in his interests, as the occult was a fashionable study at the time and many famous people pursued it. Maud Gonne herself was a member of the Golden Dawn. Bram Stoker, the author of *Dracula*, was also at one time a member. This was also a period which produced great Irish writers of gothic fiction such as Sheridan Le Fanu and Charles Maturin, who also came from the Protestant Anglo-Irish tradition.

The people involved in the Golden Dawn fully believed in real, practical magic. Among those Yeats came into contact with were Arthur Machen, the Welsh master of fantasy and horror fiction, and the famous Satanist Aleister Crowley.

Crowley used his interest and practices in magic for evil purposes and this led to what become known as the Battle of Blythe Road. As adepts, or senior members of the group, Yeats and the others refused the Satanist entry to their inner circle. Crowley was enraged and, as well as performing many rituals and spells against Yeats and the Golden Dawn, he attacked the Golden Dawn temple one night in 1900. Crowley, dressed in Highlander tartan, with a black Crusader's cross on his tunic, climbed the stairs of the temple to battle the adepts. Yeats and two other white magicians waited for him at the top, ready to use their good magic against him. When he got close enough, they kicked him down the stairs!

Yeats' interest in mysticism and the occult filtered into his work, along with a passion for Eastern art. These elements combined to make his poetry rich and filled with symbolism.

Beautiful Women

In 1891, Yeats made the first of several proposals to Maud Gonne, only to be rejected, as he was each time. During the 1890's and early 1900's, Yeats had relationships with other women, for example with the remarkable Florence Farr, a beautiful actress who he introduced to the Golden Dawn society. The women he adored were all beautiful, artistic and spirited. Ordinary women and ordinary things did not satisfy his ideals and dreams.

His first affair, however, was with Olivia Shakespear, a married writer with whom he had become friends in 1894. They had a relationship from 1896 to 1897. The affair ended when she realised that he loved only Maud Gonne. They later became friends again, after which they were lifelong correspondents. Yeats met his wife Georgie Hyde-Lees through Olivia as Georgie was Olivia's step-niece and best friend of Olivia's daughter Dorothy. Olivia also knew the American poet Ezra Pound, who had some influence on Yeats – her daughter Dorothy later married Ezra Pound.

Olivia was also friends with Florence Farr. This knot of friends and relationships gives a picture of a society of well-off, educated and artistic people who lived at a time of great change amid the pursuit of new intellectual and social freedoms.

In 1894, as a recognition of his growing literary fame, he was at last invited to visit the Gore-Booths at their beautiful house at Lissadell on the shores of Sligo Bay. In later years, after their deaths within a year of each other, he recalls his memory of the two Gore-Booth daughters, Eva and Constance, in the unforgettable verse:

> *The light of evening, Lissadell,*
> *Great windows open to the south,*
> *Two girls in silk kimonos, both*
> *Beautiful, one a gazelle.*

By his own later account, he promptly fell in love with Eva, the 'gazelle', and considered proposing to her, only to then change his mind, feeling he would be rejected by the family as a suitor.

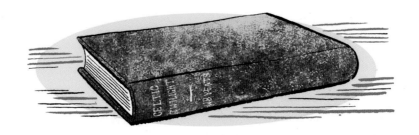

The Celtic Twilight

Yeats was a leading figure in the Irish Literary Revival, which spurred renewed interest in Irish myths and literature. In 1892, he and others founded the Irish Literary Society.

In 1893 and 1902 he published *The Celtic Twilight* in two volumes. This was a collection of folk tales told to Yeats, combined with his own visionary experiences – a world of fairies, ghosts and spirits. From this, the Celtic Literary Revival has come to be known as 'The Celtic Twilight'.

By the turn of the century, Yeats had a substantial body of work completed. His collection *The Wind Among the Reeds* (1899) contains some of his finest poems. 'The Song of the Wandering Aengus' has typical features of myth, magic, love, beauty and stunning nature imagery.

I went out to the hazel wood,
Because a fire was in my head,
And cut and peeled a hazel wand,
And hooked a berry to a thread;
And when white moths were on the wing,
And moth-like stars were flickering out,
I dropped the berry in a stream
And caught a little silver trout.

When I had laid it on the floor
I went to blow the fire a-flame,
But something rustled on the floor,
And someone called me by my name:
It had become a glimmering girl
With apple blossom in her hair
Who called me by my name and ran
And faded through the brightening air . . .

The Dramatist

At the age of 32, in the summer of 1897, Yeats stayed at Coole Park, the County Galway estate of Lady Augusta Gregory.

Lady Gregory was a writer who at the age of 41 had developed a passionate interest in the Irish language and Irish traditional culture. She was educated at home, and her future literary career was greatly influenced by the family nanny, Mary Sheridan, who was a Catholic and a native Irish speaker, and who entertained the young girl with stories of the legends and folklore of the area.

Yeats, together with Lady Gregory and her neighbour Edward Martyn, developed a plan to promote Irish drama. Edward Martyn was a playwright and a republican activist who was to become the first president of the republican party Sinn Féin in 1905. They began to stage their first productions in Dublin in 1899. Yeats' verse drama *The Countess Cathleen* was one of them, the story of a countess who sacrifices her own soul to save the poor from starvation and damnation. Later they staged Yeats' *Cathleen ni Houlihan* with Maud Gonne in the title role. This was extremely nationalistic, with Cathleen ni Houilhan, the personification of Ireland, encouraging young men to sacrifice their lives for her.

They then set up the Irish National Theatre Society with Yeats as president. They had little money to spend on the productions but one wealthy sponsor paid for the renovation of Dublin's Abbey Theatre for the company. The Abbey Theatre opened in December 1904 and put on plays by Irish playwrights including Lady Gregory. Yeats' own play *On Baile's Strand*, the first of his plays about ancient Irish hero Cúchulainn, was performed.

In 1907, they staged J.M. Synge's *The Playboy of the Western World*, which caused riots – the actors even had things thrown at them on stage – because it was considered blasphemous, it was thought to portray Irish people as violent and foolish peasants, and there was a mention of girls in their 'shifts' i.e. underdresses.

Yeats was extremely active in the company. Not only did he choose plays and hire actors and staff, but he also wrote ten plays of his own. The need to produce simple dialogue for the stage had an effect on his poetry. At this time, he gave up the elaborate lyrical work of his earlier life and adopted a harder, cleaner style.

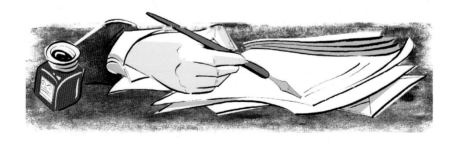

Yeats began experimenting as a playwright too. He wrote a series of plays in the style of Japanese Noh plays, to which he had been introduced by American modernist poet Ezra Pound. They were based on Irish mythology and were non-realistic. The actors wore masks and the stages were bare. Yeats called them 'plays for dancers'.

Easter 1916

On Easter Monday 1916, the poet Pádraig Pearse, socialist James Connolly and others led a rebellion in an attempt to free Ireland. One of the leaders was the Countess Markievicz – formerly Constance Gore-Booth of Sligo. Their rebellion was unsuccessful and the leaders were promptly executed, with the exception of Éamon de Valera because of his American citizenship and the Countess Markievicz because she was a woman. The executions were a miscalculation – and public opinion swung in favour of the rebels.

Although Yeats had written *Cathleen ni Houlihan* with a heroine crying out for blood sacrifice, by this time he was antagonistic to violent nationalism. His poem 'No Second Troy', written about Maud Gonne, displays what he thought of her revolutionary ideals and also how his poetry had become a melding of personal and political concerns:

> *Why should I blame her that she filled my days*
> *With misery, or that she would of late*
> *Have taught to ignorant men most violent ways*
> *Or hurled the little streets upon the great ...*

For Yeats, as for a large part of the Irish public, the Easter Rising came as a shock and a revelation. His description of the Rising in his 'Easter 1916' has become iconic and embedded in the Irish consciousness:

> All changed, changed utterly:
> A terrible beauty is born.

Of the leaders, he says:

> We know their dream; enough
> To know they dreamed and are dead;
> And what if excess of love
> Bewildered them till they died?
> I write it out in a verse—
> MacDonagh and MacBride
> And Connolly and Pearse
> Now and in time to be,
> Wherever green is worn,
> Are changed, changed utterly:
> A terrible beauty is born.

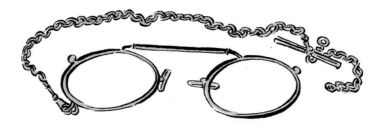

Marriage

Yeats was still pursuing Maud Gonne. He proposed to her three more times after his first attempt in 1891, with his final effort in 1917, when he was 53. In 1903, Maud had married Major John MacBride, later executed for his part in the Easter Rising of 1916. They had one son, Seán MacBride

(who became a founding member of Amnesty International). The marriage didn't last, but neither her marriage nor later his own prevented Yeats from pursuing her, which he did for about thirty years. Maud herself once commented "*You make beautiful poetry out of what you call your unhappiness, and you are happy in that*". Maud knew him well and without her as his muse, and his unrequited love to fill him with longing, he might not have penned the poetry for which he is best known. In a strange turn, driven by desperation at the rejection of his final proposal to Maud in 1917, he proposed to her daughter by Millevoye, Iseult, aged 23 at the time. Iseult also refused him.

In 1917, one month after his final rejection by Maud and then her daughter, Yeats married Georgie Hyde-Lees, aged 25 to his 53 years. Georgie quickly realised that her new husband regretted the marriage and she was afraid of losing him. She was astute, however, and knew what to do.

Georgie shared Yeats' interest in mysticism and was thought to have second sight. Shortly after they married, she began to use their shared interest in the supernatural to keep him by her side. She experimented with automatic writing, which allowed a psychic to record the messages

of spirits on paper. Yeats was fascinated and their work together on this and other mystical ideas gave him further poetic inspiration and kept the marriage together. The couple moved to Merrion Square in Dublin and had two children, Anne and Michael.

However, even while reasonably happily married, Yeats continued to have relationships with other women, a fact which Georgie knew and tolerated. He also had a close friendship with poet Dorothy Wellesley and with the journalist Edith Shackleton-Heald though she had a long-term relationship with another woman.

Later Years

Yeats' poetry had become more muscular in its language, its rhythms and its themes as he grew older. His middle poetry possesses a power that can astonish us and images that haunt us – poems such as 'The Second Coming' (1919) with its famous lines:

Turning and turning in the widening gyre
The falcon cannot hear the falconer;
Things fall apart; the centre cannot hold;
Mere anarchy is loosed upon the world . . .

And its extraordinary final image:

And what rough beast, its hour come round at last,
Slouches towards Bethlehem to be born?

He also moved towards more simplicity and directness, as in 'Sailing to Byzantium' (1926):

That is no country for old men. The young
In one another's arms, birds in the trees,
—Those dying generations—at their song . . .
The salmon-falls, the mackerel-crowded seas,
Fish, flesh, or fowl, commend all summer long
Whatever is begotten, born, and dies.
Caught in that sensual music all neglect
Monuments of unageing intellect.

In his later years his poetry also became more personal. 'The Circus Animals' Desertion' was published in the last year of his life, in his collection *Last Poems* (1939). In it the 'circus animals' stand for his own poetic inspiration and he says:

Maybe at last being but a broken man
I must be satisfied with my heart . . .

The last lines say:

Now that my ladder's gone
I must lie down where all the ladders start
In the foul rag and bone shop of the heart.

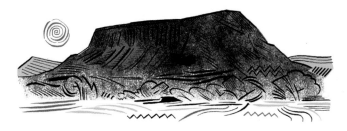

Death

Yeats' wife Georgie was at his side, together with Edith Shackleton-Heald, the last of his great loves, and his close friend Dorothy Wellesley, when he died in France on the 28th of January, 1939, having suffered from a heart condition. Nine years later his body was exhumed and buried in Sligo, which was his wish.

In County Sligo, there is a dramatic table mountain called Ben Bulben. Yeats is buried in its shadow, in Drumcliffe churchyard. His poem 'Under Ben Bulben' displays how iconic the mountain was to him and depicts his courage in the face of death. He chose his own epitaph – the closing lines of that poem:

> *Cast a cold eye*
> *On life, on death.*
> *Horseman, pass by.*

Cast a cold Eye
On Life, on Death.
Horseman, pass by.

W.B. YEATS

June 13th 1865
January 28th 1939

Places to Visit

In search of Yeats, there are many places to visit, particularly in County Sligo. A good place to start is the Yeats Memorial Building and Art Gallery in Sligo town. This is the headquarters of the International Yeats Society which runs events and keeps a library. Yeats' grave at Drumcliffe Cemetery in Drumcliffe, Sligo, is close to the iconic table mountain Ben Bulben.

Other places of interest include Pollexfen House in Sligo town, the home of Yeats' maternal relatives; Elsinore House in Rosses Point, Sligo, which also belonged to Yeats' maternal relatives and where he spent summer holidays; Lissadell House and Gardens, the home of the Gore Booths; the lovely Sally Gardens, Ballysadare, Sligo; and the Isle of Innisfree, Lough Gill, Sligo.

Timeline

13th June 1865 W. B. Yeats is born in Dublin

1865 American Civil War ends

1867 Fenian uprising

1867 Yeats family moves to London

1872 – 1874 Susan Yeats and children live in Sligo

1874 Yeats family returns to London – children home-schooled

Irish Home Rule movement starts

1877 W.B. Yeats starts at Godolphin School

1879 – 1882 Irish Land War

1881 Yeats family moves to Dublin

1884 W.B. Yeats starts at Metropolitan School of Art, Dublin

1885 Yeats first poems published in *Dublin University Review*

1886 First Irish Home Rule Bill rejected by the British House of Commons

1887 Yeats family moves back to London

W.B. Yeats meets occultist Madame Blavatska

1888 Jack the Ripper murders in London

1889 Yeats publishes first major work: *The Wanderings of Oisin and Other Poems*

Yeats meets Maud Gonne

1890 Yeats joins The Hermetic Order of the Golden Dawn

1891 Yeats first marriage proposal to Maud Gonne

Death of Charles Stewart Parnell, Uncrowned King of Ireland

1892 Yeats co-founds the Irish Literary Society

1893 World's first full women's suffrage enacted in New Zealand

1895 Trial of Oscar Wilde

1897 Yeats joins with Lady Gregory and Edward Martyn to plan and promote new and native Irish drama

1897 Bram Stoker's *Dracula* is published

1899 Yeats first dramatic productions presented in Dublin

1990 W. B. Yeats' mother Susan dies

1901 First Nobel Prizes awarded

1903 World's first controlled flight by the Wright Brothers

1904 Abbey Theatre opens in December

1907 J.M. Synge's controversial work *The Playboy of the Western World* is performed in the Abbey

1913 Union strike in Dublin known as Dublin Lockout

1914 Government of Ireland Act granting Home Rule passed but postponed due to conflict in Europe

1914 – 1918 World War I

1916 Easter Rising

1917 Yeats' final marriage proposal to Maud Gonne rejected

Yeats marries Georgie Hyde-Lees

Russian revolution

1919 First Irish Dáil (parliament) and Irish War of Independence

1921 Anglo-Irish Treaty with Britain for 26-county Free State with 6-county Northern Ireland

Adolf Hitler becomes Führer of Nazi party

1922 W. B. Yeats' father John dies

1922 – 1923 Irish Civil War

1923 Yeats the first Irishman awarded Nobel Prize in Literature

1922 – 1928 Yeats serves as Senator in the Irish Free State

1924 Yeats chairs committee on designs of first Irish currency

1925	Mussolini becomes dictator of Italy
1927	Stalin becomes leader of the Soviet Union
	First 'talkie' movie released – *The Jazz Singer*
1929	Wall Street Crash; start of American Great Depression
1932	Franklin D. Roosevelt becomes U.S. President
1934	Hitler declares himself Führer of Germany
1936 – 1939	Spanish Civil War
1937	First Irish Constitution – replacement of Irish Free State with sovereign nation of Ireland
28th January 1939	W. B. Yeats dies in France of heart condition
1st September 1939	Beginning of World War II